SESAME STREET

SIGN LANGUAGE FUN

SIGN LANGUAGE FUN

With LINDA BOVE

Illustrated by Tom Cooke

Featuring Jim Henson's Sesame Street Muppets

Prepared in Cooperation with the National Theatre of the Deaf

Random House / Children's Television Workshop

Library of Congress Cataloging in Publication Data:

Main entry under title: Sesame Street sign language fun. SUMMARY: Presents in sign language words grouped in such categories as the family, school, colors, playground, seasons, utensils and food, woods, transportation, jungle, and feelings and emotions. 1. Sign language—Juvenile literature. [1. Sign language] I. Sesame Street.
HV2476.S47   419   79-5570
ISBN 0-394-84212-X (trade); 0-394-94212-4 (lib. bdg.)
Manufactured in the United States of America   9 0

Note to Parents

Sign language is a beautiful and expressive way to communicate that both children and adults will find intriguing. *Sign Language Fun* is an introduction to sign language, a word book, and a picture book. Like the *Sesame Street* television show, *Sign Language Fun* includes concepts such as opposites, action words, and feelings, all delightfully illustrated with the Sesame Street Muppets. Photographs on every page show Linda Bove demonstrating the sign for each word, so your hands will find plenty of familiar topics to "talk" about.

You may want to help your child imitate the hand positions in the photographs. Arrows are used on some pictures to show you how to move your hands or fingers. When you sign words, say them aloud and use facial expressions to help convey the meaning.

About Linda Bove

Linda is an actress who is deaf. She is a regular, long-time cast member of *Sesame Street* and has been sharing her signing and theatrical talents with viewers. She has also been seen on the television shows *Happy Days* and *Search for Tomorrow* and is an associate of the National Theatre of the Deaf. Linda has put together this unique picture book with the help of her *Sesame Street* friends for any child or parent who enjoys discovering and describing the world in new ways.

In the Morning

Good

morning

alarm clock

bed

window

sunrise

toothpaste

toothbrush

wake up

comb

cup

mirror

Good

morning!

It's time

  to get up.

mother

father

baby

brother

sister

The Family

family

mother

father

baby

brother

sister

dog

cat

fish

grandmother, grandfather

dog

cat

grandmother

grandfather

fish

School Days

school

teacher

book

scissors

chair

student

children   read

write   paint

door

How many things in this picture can you "sign"?

I

want

to read

a book

about

cookies.

colors

Colors

red

blue

yellow

green

squeeze fist

orange

white

black

purple

pink

brown

On the Farm

farm

cow

horse

pig

rooster

feed the horse.

Playground Fun

playground

ball

slide

friend

jump rope

swing

seesaw

balloon

How many things in this picture can you "sign"?

Come   play

with   me.

Things That Are Opposite

opposites

up

down

push

pull

in

out

big

little

over

under

hot

cold

old

young

Action Words

action

jump

walk

run

climb

stand

sit

kneel

How many things in this picture can you "sign"?

I can jump very high.

I
can
jump

very

high.

People in the Neighborhood

neighborhood

grocer

policeman

letter carrier

sanitation worker

plumber

dentist

barber

How many things in this picture can you "sign"?

Don't   cross

the street

when

make fist

the traffic light is red!

Spring

spring

bird

flowers

raincoat

grass

shoes

butterfly

rain

umbrella

T-shirt

Summer

summer

sun

boat

dive

swim

hot

beach

bathing suit

dig

water

Autumn

autumn

leaves

ride bicycle

roller skates

rake

tree

kite

coat

wind

Winter

winter

snow

ice

ice skate

sled

snowball

mitten

scarf

hat

Utensils and Food

food

table

knife

fork

spoon

glass

soup

milk

napkin

cookies

peanut butter

jelly

sandwich

How many things in this picture can you "sign"?

I am thirsty.

Where is the milk?

woods

In the Woods

deer

owl

rabbit

turtle

fox

raccoon

skunk

spider

squirrel

frog

bear

How many things in this picture can you "sign"?

Who

lives

in

the woods?

transportation

How People Get Around

car

airplane

train

rocket

motorcycle

bus

truck

helicopter

How many things in this picture can you "sign"?

Do

you

like

to ride   a motorcycle?

jungle

In the Jungle

monkey

giraffe

lion

rhinoceros

elephant

tiger

crocodile

mouse

snake

hippopotamus

How many things in this picture can you "sign"?

Can

you

find

the mouse?

The Way You Feel

feelings

happy

sad

surprise

frightened

shy

angry

love

brave

excited

bored

proud

Nighttime

Good night.

moon

sleep

dreams

stars

yawn

How many things in this picture can you "sign"?

Good night!

Have   sweet   dreams.

1

2

3

4

5

6

7

8

9

10

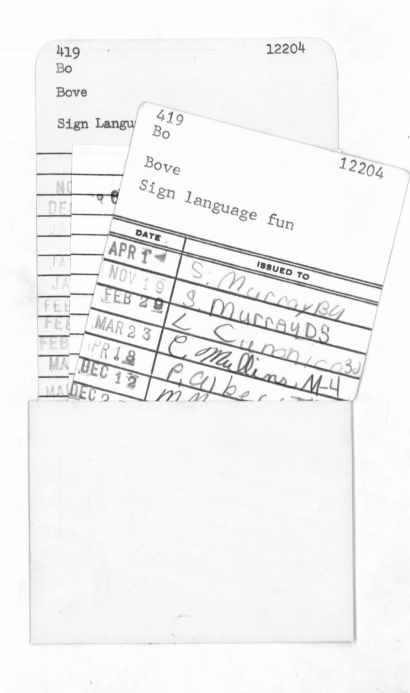